D1482871

My United States

California

LAUREN NEWMAN

Children's Press®
An Imprint of Scholastic Inc.

Content Consultant

James Wolfinger, PhD, Associate Dean and Professor
College of Education, DePaul University, Chicago, Illinois

Library of Congress Cataloging-in-Publication Data
Names: Newman, Lauren, author.
Title: California / by Lauren Newman.
Description: New York : Children's Press, an imprint of Scholastic Inc., [2018] | Series: A true book |
   Includes bibliographical references and index.
Identifiers: LCCN 2016058680l ISBN 9780531252529 (library binding : alkaline paper) | ISBN
   9780531232828 (paperback : alkaline paper)
Subjects: LCSH: California—Juvenile literature.
Classification: LCC F861.3 .N49 2018 | DDC 979.4—dc23
LC record available at https://lccn.loc.gov/2016058680

Photographs ©: cover: Vacclav/Dreamstime; back cover ribbon: AliceLiddelle/Getty Images; back cover bottom: Mathew Sumner/ZUMA Press/Newscom; 3 map: Jim McMahon; 3 bottom: stone18/iStockphoto; 4 bottom: Billy Hustace/Getty Images; 4 top: Virginie Miramon/Water Rights/Superstock, Inc.; 5 top: Russ Bishop/Alamy Images; 5 bottom: photomaster/Shutterstock; 6 inset: Vacclav/Dreamstime; 7 top: AA World Travel Library/Alamy Images; 7 center: FrozenShutter/iStockphoto; 7 bottom: Sergio Pitamitz/age fotostock; 8-9: Ron_Thomas/iStockphoto; 11: Russ Bishop/Alamy Images; 12: LICreate/iStockphoto; 13 main: Russ Bishop/age fotostock; 13 icons: Okashi/Shutterstock; 14: Panoramic Images/Getty Images; 15: Russ Bishop/Alamy Images; 16-17: Adonis Villanueva/Shutterstock; 19: Robyn Beck/AFP/Getty Images; 20: Robot100/Dreamstime; 22 left: Svetocheck/Shutterstock; 22 right: Brothers Good/Shutterstock; 23 center right: studiocasper/iStockphoto; 23 top right: Virginie Miramon/Water Rights/Superstock, Inc.; 23 top left: photomaster/Shutterstock; 23 bottom left: robertcicchetti/iStockphoto; 23 bottom right: Harry Taylor/Getty Images; 23 top center: Panoramic Images/Getty Images; 24-25: Morton Kunstler/National Geographic/Getty Images; 27: The Granger Collection; 29: North Wind Picture Archives/Alamy Images; 30 left: Viktorcvetkovic/iStockphoto; 30 right: Photo Researchers, Inc/Alamy Images; 31 center: Circa Images/Glasshouse Images/Superstock, Inc.; 31 left: Svetocheck/Shutterstock; 31 right: Vacclav/Dreamstime; 32: Alexander Alland, Jr./Getty Images; 33: Arthur Schatz/The LIFE Pcture Collection/Getty Images; 34-35: Mel Melcon/Los Angeles Times/Getty Images; 36: Makena Stock Media/Design Pics Inc/Alamy Images; 37: Billy Hustace/Getty Images; 38: danbreckwoldt/iStockphoto; 39 main: serg3d/iStockphoto; 39 inset: Neil Godwin/MacLife Magazine/Getty Images; 40 background: PepitoPhotos/iStockphoto; 40 bottom right: FOODCOLLECTION/age fotostock; 41: Steve Silvas/Getty Images; 42 top left: Album/Superstock, Inc.; 42 top right: NYPL/Science Source/Getty Images; 42 bottom left: Adrian Sherratt/Alamy Images; 42 bottom right: ZUMA Press Inc./Alamy Images; 43 top left: Anthony Harvey/Photoshot/Everett Collection; 43 top right: ZUMA Press Inc./Alamy Images; 43 center left: NASA/The LIFE Picture Collection/Getty Images; 43 bottom left: ZUMA Press Inc./Alamy Images; 43 bottom center: Jerry Colli/Dreamstime; 43 bottom right: Boris Streubel/ullstein bild/Getty Images; 44 top: Design Pics/Deb Garside/Getty Images; 44 bottom left: Balint Roxana/Alamy Images; 44 bottom right: Marc Venema/Shutterstock; 45 top: Everett Historical/Shutterstock; 45 center: meltonmedia/Shutterstock; 45 bottom: Mel Melcon/Los Angeles Times/Getty Images.

Maps by Map Hero, Inc.

Front cover: The Golden Gate Bridge
Back cover: A surfer

Welcome to California

←California

Find the Truth!

Everything you are about to read is true **except** for one of the sentences on this page.

Which one is **TRUE**?

T or F California is home to the longest mural in the world.

T or F The first European explorers to visit California were British.

Find the answers in this book.

3

Contents

Map: This Is California! 6

1 Land and Wildlife
What is the terrain of California
like and what lives there? 9

2 Government
What are the different parts
of California's government? 17

THE BIG TRUTH!

Golden
poppy

What Represents California?
What designs, objects, plants, and
animals symbolize California?. 22

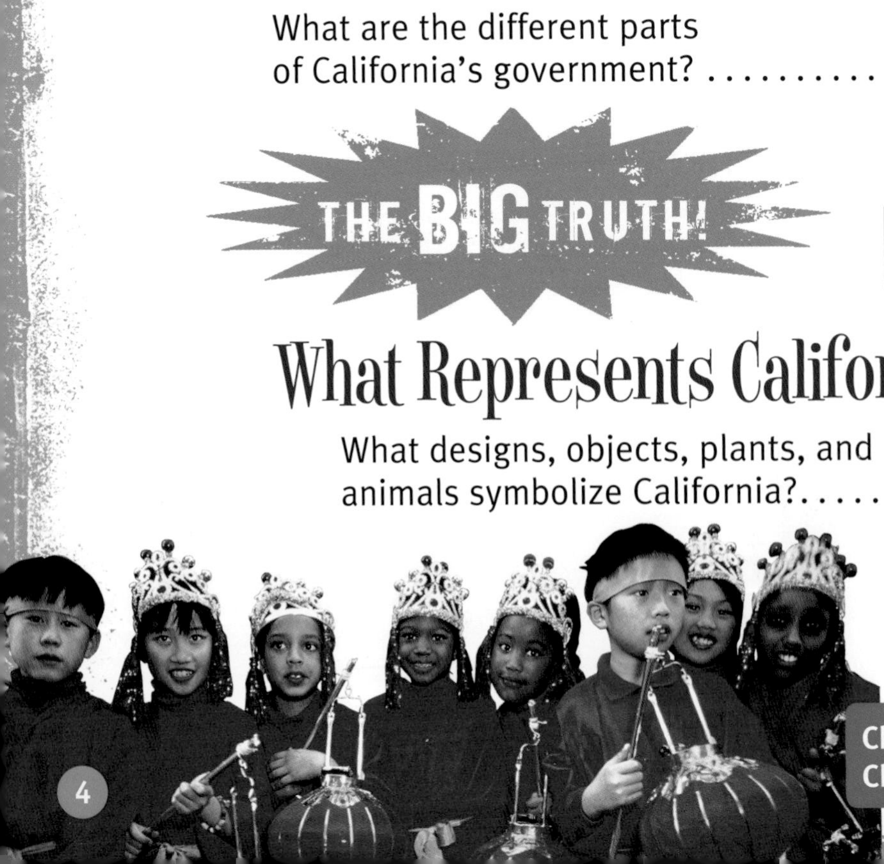

Children celebrate
Chinese New Year

4

Sea lions rest on a buoy

3 History

How did California become
the state it is today? 25

4 Culture

What do Californians do for work and fun? 35

Famous People 42

Did You Know That 44

Resources 46

Important Words 47

Index 48

About the Author 48

California valley quail

This Is California!

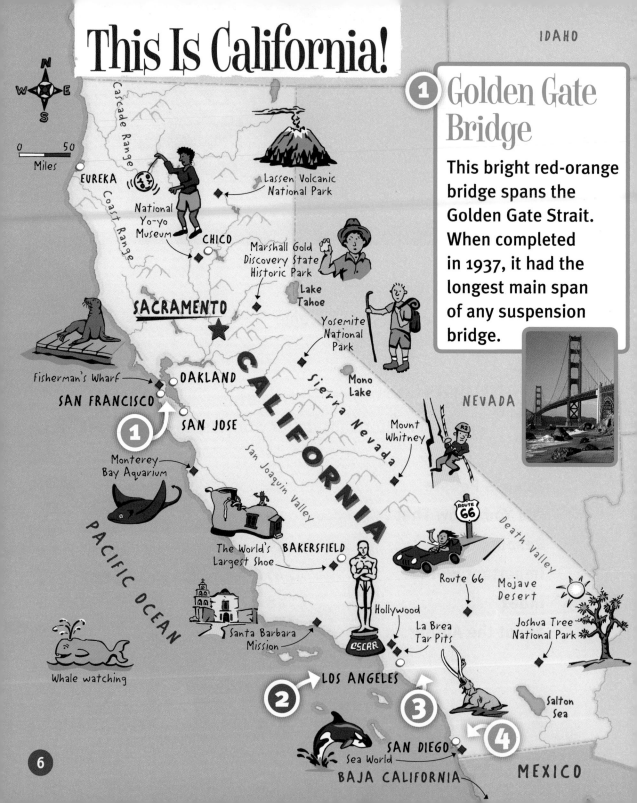

IDAHO

N W E S

0 50 Miles

EUREKA

Cascade Range

Coast Range

Lassen Volcanic National Park

National Yo-yo Museum

CHICO

Marshall Gold Discovery State Historic Park

Lake Tahoe

SACRAMENTO

Yosemite National Park

CALIFORNIA

Sierra Nevada

Mono Lake

Mount Whitney

NEVADA

① Golden Gate Bridge

① Golden Gate Bridge

This bright red-orange bridge spans the Golden Gate Strait. When completed in 1937, it had the longest main span of any suspension bridge.

Fisherman's Wharf

OAKLAND

SAN FRANCISCO

① SAN JOSE

Monterey Bay Aquarium

PACIFIC OCEAN

San Joaquin Valley

The World's Largest Shoe

BAKERSFIELD

ROUTE 66

Route 66

Death Valley

Mojave Desert

Joshua Tree National Park

Santa Barbara Mission

Hollywood OSCAR

La Brea Tar Pits

Whale watching

② LOS ANGELES

③

④

Salton Sea

SAN DIEGO

Sea World

BAJA CALIFORNIA

MEXICO

6

② Los Angeles

This city features attractions ranging from the star-studded Hollywood Walk of Fame to the ancient La Brea Tar Pits. Take a walk along the sandy beaches or view the Hollywood sign up close.

COLORADO

③ Disneyland Resort

Located in Anaheim, outside of Los Angeles, Disneyland is the first of the Disney Company's theme parks. It attracts more than 14 million visitors from around the world each year.

ZONA

④ San Diego Zoo

Visit the San Diego Zoo to see more than 3,500 animals and more than 700,000 plants from around the world. The organization includes an institute that protects animals and environments in the wild.

NEW MEXICO

California has the third-longest coastline of any state in the country, at 840 miles (1,350 kilometers).

CHAPTER 1

Land and Wildlife

From soaring mountains to deep valleys, sunny beaches and sizzling deserts, California has everything. This beautiful state lies on the west coast of the United States. It is big, too. California is the nation's third-largest state in area. It's also big in population, with more than 39 million people, the most of any state. Many people live in or visit California to experience its **diverse** wildlife, awesome landscapes, and nearly perfect climate.

Highs and Lows

California's geography is extreme. Climb 14,505 feet (4,421 meters) to the top of Mount Whitney, the highest point in the **contiguous** United States. Or descend into Death Valley, the continent's lowest spot, at 282 feet (86 m) below sea level.

California's western coast has steep cliffs and sandy beaches. East of this, the central valley has fertile farmland.

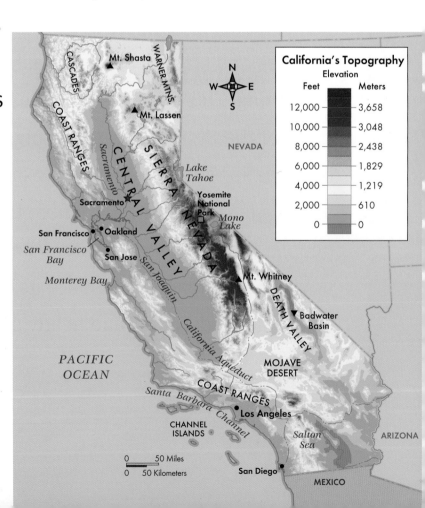

California's Topography

Elevation

Feet	Meters
12,000	3,658
10,000	3,048
8,000	2,438
6,000	1,829
4,000	1,219
2,000	610
0	0

Yosemite National Park

Nestled in the Yosemite Valley is Yosemite National Park. People visit the park to see its amazing rock formations and towering sequoia trees. Gushing waterfalls are found all over the park too. One waterfall is Yosemite Falls (pictured here), which is thought to be the tallest waterfall in North America! Yosemite National Park is also home to over 400 kinds of animals. Some animals found in the park are coyotes, great gray owls, and black bears.

Death Valley is famous for its desert climate and landscape.

East of the valley are the towering Sierra Nevada mountains, home to Mount Whitney. This is California's highest point at 14,505 feet (4,421 meters). To the southeast, the deserts are hot and dry. The Mojave Desert's Death Valley is the world's hottest spot and North America's driest and lowest. Its record temperature is 134°F (56.7°C). Annual rainfall is a tiny 2.4 inches (6 centimeters), and it sits 282 feet (86 m) below sea level.

Climate

Packing for a trip to California can be tricky. The state has several different climate zones, each with its own temperatures and **precipitation**. Southern California is mild year-round, averaging about 69°F (21°C) in summer and 57°F (14°C) in winter. Northern California is slightly cooler. Southern California sees little rain, while Northern California sees more. The state's mountains get plenty of snow.

MAXIMUM TEMPERATURE
134°F

MINIMUM TEMPERATURE
-45°F

A skier enjoys fresh snow in California.

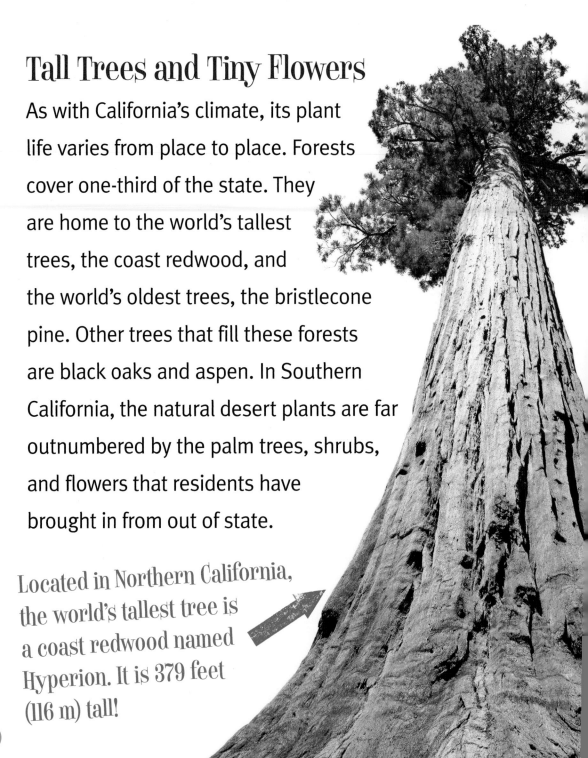

Tall Trees and Tiny Flowers

As with California's climate, its plant life varies from place to place. Forests cover one-third of the state. They are home to the world's tallest trees, the coast redwood, and the world's oldest trees, the bristlecone pine. Other trees that fill these forests are black oaks and aspen. In Southern California, the natural desert plants are far outnumbered by the palm trees, shrubs, and flowers that residents have brought in from out of state.

Located in Northern California, the world's tallest tree is a coast redwood named Hyperion. It is 379 feet (116 m) tall!

Sea lions rest on a buoy in Ventura Harbor, located in Ventura, California.

California Creatures

California is home to a diverse range of animals. Common animals found throughout the state are squirrels, foxes, and deer. Bobcats, black bears, and cougars roam the forests and mountains. The desert showcases animals such as lizards and rattlesnakes. The coast is home to sea lions and otters. In the winter, people like to watch for gray whales that **migrate** from Alaska to the warm ocean waters off of Southern California. Birds of all types make California their home.

It took 14 years to build California's capitol building.

CHAPTER

Government

California has had several capitals. While still under Spain's control, the region's center of government was in Monterey. When it became a state, California chose the growing city of Pueblo de San Jose as its capital. Then over the next few years, the capital moved from Vallejo to Benecia and finally to Sacramento in 1854. Despite a few attempts to move the capital again, it's stayed in Sacramento ever since.

State Government Basics

Government's most important job is to protect and serve the citizens and the environment. California's government is divided into three branches. The governor heads the executive branch, which enforces the state's laws. The legislative branch, through the Senate and the Assembly, writes the laws. These laws are interpreted by the judicial branch, which is made up of the state's courts. Together, these branches keep California safe and running smoothly.

CALIFORNIA'S STATE GOVERNMENT

LEGISLATIVE BRANCH	EXECUTIVE BRANCH	JUDICIAL BRANCH
Makes and passes state laws	**Carries out state laws**	**Enforces state laws**

LEGISLATIVE BRANCH

Senate (40 members)	Assembly (80 members)

EXECUTIVE BRANCH

Executive Branch Members:
Governor, Secretary of State,
Lieutenant Governor, Treasurer,
Attorney General

Cabinet

Departments of:
Education, Environmental Protection,
Food and Agriculture, Labor,
and many others

JUDICIAL BRANCH

Supreme Court

Courts of Appeal
(6 with 19 divisions)

Superior
Courts
(58)

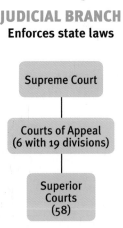

At election time, Californians often vote on issues. Signs like these try to persuade people how to cast their votes.

Voter Power

Voters have a lot of direct power on the laws and practices of California. In many states, voters elect representatives to propose and decide on new laws and revisions to the constitution. Californians often propose and vote on these issues directly. People also have the right to remove an elected official from office, including the governor. This happened in 2003, when voters removed Governor Gray Davis from office and replaced him with Arnold Schwarzenegger.

California's National Role

Every state has members in U.S. Congress. Each state, including California, has two senators. The number of representatives in the House of Representatives depends on a state's population. California has 53, the most of any state.

Each state also has a certain number of votes to apply in the election of the U.S. president. These electoral votes are equal to the number of members of Congress. With 2 senators and 53 representatives, California has 55 electoral votes.

With more electoral votes than any other state, California plays a big role in presidential elections!

2 senators and 53 representatives

55 electoral votes

Representing California

Elected officials in California represent a population with a range of interests, lifestyles, and backgrounds.

Ethnicity (2015 estimates)

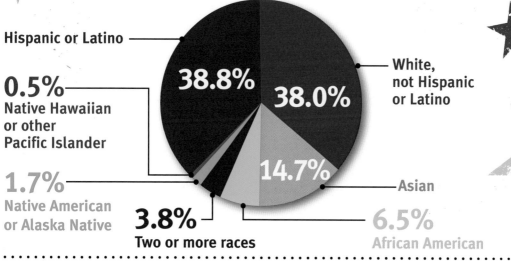

Hispanic or Latino — **38.8%**

White, not Hispanic or Latino — **38.0%**

0.5%
Native Hawaiian or other Pacific Islander

1.7%
Native American or Alaska Native

3.8%
Two or more races

14.7% Asian

6.5%
African American

1/3 of the population have a degree beyond high school.

50% own their own homes.

87% live in cities.

27% of Californians were born in other countries.

80% of the population graduated high school.

1.8 million Californians are military veterans.

What Represents California?

States choose specific animals, plants, and objects to represent the values and characteristics of the land and its people. Find out why these symbols were chosen to represent California or discover surprising curiosities about them.

Seal

The woman is Minerva, the Roman goddess of wisdom. The river is the Sacramento and the mountains are the Sierra Nevadas. The small miner represents the Gold Rush of 1849 that brought thousands of people to California. Eureka is Greek for "I have found it!"

Flag

The grizzly bear on the flag is California's state animal. This "Bear Flag" became the state flag in 1911.

California Valley Quail

STATE BIRD

This plump little quail is known for its hardiness and its ability to adapt.

California Redwood

STATE TREE

These giant trees are not fully mature until they are 400 to 500 years old.

Golden Poppy

STATE FLOWER

This bright bloom is also called the flame flower and *copa de oro*, Spanish for "cup of gold." Californians celebrate Poppy Day every April 6th.

Gold

STATE MINERAL

In honor of the Gold Rush of 1849, gold is the state mineral. California is still home to a few prospectors panning for gold.

Calfiornia Grizzly Bear

STATE ANIMAL

Several thousand of these bears once roamed California, but humans wiped them out. No California grizzlies have been seen since 1924.

Benitoite

STATE MINERAL

This rare "blue diamond" was named after the San Benito River, near where it was discovered.

Spanish explorers look out over what is now called San Francisco Bay.

History

A Spanish novelist once wrote about a land called California that was ruled by a fierce queen named Califia. Back in the 1500s, some Europeans thought this story was true. They wanted to find this land filled with great treasures. Califia's land was never found, of course. But when explorers happened upon this region of soaring mountains and beautiful coastline, they called it California. This is how the state was named.

Native Americans

California's history dates back more than 11,000 years! The first explorers crossed a temporary land bridge from Asia into what is now Alaska and spread across North America. Over the next several thousand years, many different Native American cultures

This map shows the approximate areas where different Native American groups were living when Europeans arrived.

developed. As many as 300,000 Native Americans were living in California before European settlers arrived. They belong to hundreds of large family groups called clans. The clans spoke many different languages and had different belief systems.

Clans such as the Tipai-Itai of Southern California survived by hunting and gathering wild foods. Their food included cactus and acorns. Other groups were skilled at agriculture. For example, the Mojave raised corn, beans, and squash. They had easy access to fresh water from the Colorado River. The Chumash lived on the coast. They were expert shipbuilders and fishers. Like many Native American groups, the Karok people in the north built houses made of plants. The north's Pomo were skilled basket makers.

Yuma men pose for a photo.

European Exploration

The first Europeans to spot what is now California were the Spanish in 1542. They claimed the land but built no permanent settlement. Then, starting in the 1760s, Spain worried that other European countries would claim the land. It sent expeditions to California to build military forts and **missions**. They hoped to **convert** the Native Americans to Christianity. They also hoped native groups would work farms and ranches, and help them resist settlement by other Europeans.

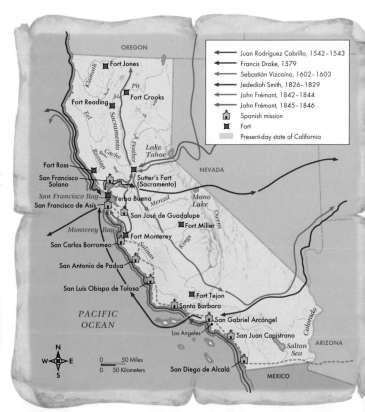

This map shows the routes explorers from Europe took through California.

Spanish settlers built 21 missions up and down the California coast.

In those early days of settlement, many Native Americans died of diseases brought by the Spanish. Others died during conflicts with Spanish soldiers. The region passed to Mexico when the **colony** gained independence from Spain in 1821. Life for Native Americans, however, did not improve. Only about 100,000 survived by 1840.

White Americans and settlers from Europe and Asia began entering California in increasing numbers in 1841. Within decades, Native Americans were forced onto dry and isolated **reservations**. Reservation life remains challenging today.

Road to Statehood

In 1846, white American settlers fought Mexico in the Bear Flag Revolt. The Americans won, and California was briefly an independent nation. By January 1847, however, the United States had claimed it as a **territory**. The following year, gold was discovered. People poured in from around the world. A few struck it rich panning for gold. Others made money selling supplies to the miners.

Timeline of California Events

9000 BCE
People first settle in what is now California.

1846
The Bear Flag Revolt briefly establishes California as its own country.

9000 BCE	1760s CE	1846	1848

1760s CE
Spain begins building missions and forts in California.

CALIFORNIA REPUBLIC

1848
The gold rush begins, bringing thousands of settlers to California.

Modern California

The gold rush pushed California toward statehood.
On September 9, 1850, it became the 31st state.
At the time, war was brewing among Americans.
Activists, many of them in the North, wanted to end
slavery. Southern plantation owners wanted to keep
it. When the Civil War broke out in 1861, California
sided with the North. The state contributed supplies
and soldiers until the North won in 1865.

1937
Workers complete the
Golden Gate Bridge,
connecting San Francisco
with its neighbors across
the Golden Gate Strait.

Sept. 9, 1850
California becomes
a state.

1850

1906

1937

2011

1906
A massive earthquake hits
San Francisco, killing an
estimated 3,000 people.

2011
A dry period kicks off a
drought that would last
nearly six years.

People continued to pour into California. In the 1930s, agricultural workers arrived, fleeing failing farms and economic troubles facing the rest of the country. In the 1940s, aircraft and shipbuilding industries grew. They supplied the United States and its allies during World War II (1939–1945). After the war, researchers from Europe moved to California. This established a reputation for research and technology there that the state still has today.

When the transcontinental railroad was completed in 1869, getting to California became a lot easier.

Changing Workers' Lives

Agriculture has long been a backbone of California's economy. Throughout the state's history, however, agriculture workers have often been treated unfairly and paid little. A Mexican American activist named César Chávez (1927–1993) began to change that. His family had moved to California in 1939 looking for agricultural work after losing their farm in Arizona. Beginning in the 1950s, Chávez led huge peaceful protests and eventually formed a **union**. This union later became part of the United Farm Workers of America, one of the biggest unions in the United States today.

With a length of 2,754 feet (840 m), *The Great Wall of Los Angeles* is the longest mural in the world!

CHAPTER 4

Culture

California has a lively and booming culture. Art is a big part of that. Many of the movies you watch are probably products of Hollywood's film industry. Art is also found in California's streets and museums. A **mural** called *The Great Wall of Los Angeles* celebrates that city's diversity. California has sparked the imagination of many writers, too, such as Amy Tan and Jack London.

Surfers flock to California's coast to take advantage of the Pacific Ocean's waves.

California at Play

Sports and recreation play a large role in shaping California's culture. Locals love to be outdoors. Because the climate is so mild and the days so sunny, many Californians like to surf, hike, and go camping.

Several sports teams call California home. Professional teams include the Los Angeles Dodgers, the Los Angeles Lakers, and the San Francisco 49ers. Whether it's baseball, basketball, football, hockey, or soccer, California has it all!

Celebration, California Style

Californians know how to celebrate. In Pasadena, people kick off the New Year with the Tournament of Roses. This parade features beautiful and complicated floats decorated entirely in flowers. A few weeks later, the Chinatown neighborhood in Los Angeles marks the Chinese New Year with a two-day celebration. Los Angeles also hosts big Cinco de Mayo (in May) and Dia de los Muertos (in November) festivities. If you're a film fan, check out Hollywood's Academy Awards each February!

Children celebrate Chinese New Year in San Francisco's Chinatown, the largest Chinese community in the United States.

At Work

California has a huge, thriving economy. One-third of California is devoted to farmland. The state's biggest crops are nuts and fruits, such as almonds, walnuts, oranges, and grapes. California is also the United States' leader in manufacturing computers. This is where the company Apple started. People in California work in education, health services, and science, as well. Of course, because California is home to Hollywood, many Californians are involved in filmmaking.

The Hollywood neighborhood in Los Angeles is marked with a giant sign.

On the Cutting Edge

Silicon Valley near San Francisco is home to most of the country's computer companies. They are changing the world with their products. The companies include huge, established corporations such as Apple and Google. There are also many startups, or small companies that are just starting out. All these businesses constantly explore new ideas, creating a variety of new jobs and technologies.

On the Table

California's coastal location and sunny climate ensure a fresh supply of seafood, fruits, and vegetables. The state's mix of people adds to the variety of foods that residents eat and grow. One example is the California roll, a twist on traditional Japanese sushi. Mexican food is also popular in California. Tamales and tacos are common across the state.

 ## Chicken Tacos

Ask an adult to help you!

This recipe calls for chicken, but you can use any meat—or no meat!

Ingredients
1 ½ pounds of chicken breast
½ teaspoon each of salt, black pepper, and chili powder
2 teaspoons ground cumin
olive oil to cook chicken

½ red onion, diced
½ head red cabbage, chopped
2 tomatoes, diced
Cilantro and fresh lime juice to taste
Small soft tortillas

Directions
1. Season the chicken with salt, black pepper, chili powder, and cumin.
2. With an adult's help, cook the chicken thoroughly in a skillet. Its internal temperature should be at least 165 degrees Fahrenheit (74 degrees Celsius).
3. Cut the chicken into cubes or strips.
4. Add chicken, onion, cabbage, tomatoes, and cilantro to taste to each tortilla. Squeeze on a bit of fresh lime to finish!

A Diverse State

California is a popular and vibrant place. It is a place where many people want to live and visit because of its beautiful climate, dazzling environment, unique mix of people, and rich history. These elements have helped shape California into the

Skateboarders are a regular sight at California parks and beaches.

amazing state it is today. Few states can rival the range of experiences that California has to offer. ★

Famous People

Walt Disney

(1901–1966) produced the first feature-length animated film, *Snow White and the Seven Dwarfs*, and created the beloved character Mickey Mouse.

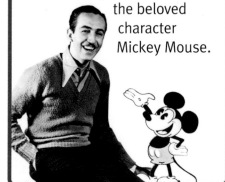

Jonas Salk

(1914–1995) was a doctor and researcher who invented the vaccine (a treatment that helps prevent a disease) for polio in 1955. He founded the Salk Institute for Biological Studies in San Diego.

Nancy Pelosi

(1940–) is a politician. She served as Speaker of the House, or leader of the U.S. House of Representatives, from 2007 to 2011. She was the first woman in U.S. history to do so.

Maya Angelou

(1928–2014) was a writer best known for her poetry and memoirs, especially *I Know Why the Caged Bird Sings*. She spent part of her childhood and early adulthood in California.

George Lucas

(1944–) is a filmmaker from Modesto. He is best known for creating the *Star Wars* series.

Judith Baca

(1946–) is an artist and educator in Los Angeles. She created the mural *The Great Wall of Los Angeles*.

Sally Ride

(1951–2012) was an astronaut who became the first American woman in space. She later worked to inspire kids, especially girls, to study science. She was born in Encino.

Steve Jobs

(1955–2011) was a cofounder of the Apple computer company. He was born in San Francisco.

Earvin "Magic" Johnson

(1959–) is a basketball player who won five NBA championships during his 13 seasons with the Los Angeles Lakers.

Michelle Kwan

(1980–) is the most successful figure skater in U.S. history. She won nine U.S. and five world championships. She is also a gold and silver medalist in the Olympics.

Did You Know That...

Grizzly bears were so common in California that the state was once nicknamed the Grizzly Bear State. As the human population shot up in the 1800s, however, the state's bear population shot down. By the 1920s, the grizzly bear was extinct in California.

The entire state of Rhode Island could fit inside California more than 130 times.

 Roughly 1 in 8 Americans lives in California.

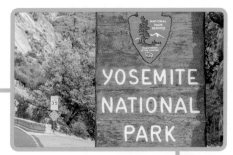

California is home to 28 National Park Service areas, including forests, trails, historic sites, monuments, and other important places.

In 1848, after the Mexican-American War, the United States gained nearly half of Mexico's land. This area now makes up all or part of seven states, including California.

Experts estimate that nearly 44 percent of Californians speak a language other than English at home.

¡Hola!
你好

Hass avocados are the most common type of avocados sold in U.S. stores. Though grown in many parts of the world, all Hass avocado trees are descendants of a single tree grown in California.

Did you find the truth?

(T) California is home to the longest mural in the world.

(F) The first European explorers to visit California were British.

Resources

Books

Benoit, Peter. *The California Gold Rush*. New York: Children's Press, 2013.

Orr, Tamra B. *California*. New York: Children's Press, 2014.

Movies

Alvin and the Chipmunks and its sequels (2007, 2009, 2011, and 2015)

Alexander and the Terrible, Horrible, No Good, Very Bad Day (2014)

Back to the Future I, II, and *III* (1985, 1989, 1990)

Finding Dory (2016)

Freaky Friday (2003)

The Karate Kid (1984)

The Muppets (2011)

Pee Wee's Big Adventure (1985)

The Sandlot (1993)

Singin' in the Rain (1952)

Stand and Deliver (1988)

Who Framed Roger Rabbit? (1988)

Visit this Scholastic website for more information on California:

★ www.factsfornow.scholastic.com
Enter the keyword **California**

Important Words

colony (KAH-luh-nee) a settlement formed by people from a foreign country

contiguous (kuhn-TIHG-yoo-uhs) touching along a common boundary; the contiguous United States includes all states except Hawai'i and Alaska

convert (kuhn-VURT) to change one's religion or other beliefs

diverse (di-VURS) having many different types or kinds

migrate (MYE-grate) to move from one country or area to another

missions (MISH-uhnz) churches or other places where people sent to a foreign country to teach about their religion live and work

mural (MYOOR-uhl) a large painting done on a wall

precipitation (pri-sip-uh-TAY-shuhn) the falling of water from the sky in the form of rain, sleet, hail, or snow

reservations (rez-ur-VAY-shuhnz) areas of land set aside by the government for a special purpose

territory (TER-uh-tor-ee) an area owned by the United States that is not a state

union (YOON-yuhn) an organized group of workers set up to help improve such things as working conditions, wages, and health benefits

Index

Page numbers in **bold** indicate illustrations.

agriculture, 27, 28, 32, 33, 38, **45**
animals, **7**, 11, **15**, **23**, **44**
art, **34–35**, **43**

Bear Flag Revolt, 30

capital city, **16–17**
celebrations, **37**
Chinatown, **37**
climate, 12, **13**, 31, 36, 40
coastline, **8–9**, 10, 15, **36**
computer companies, 38, 39, 43

Death Valley, 10, **12**
Disneyland Resort, **7**
drought, 31

earthquakes, **31**
elections, **19**, 20
elevation, **10**, 12
ethnic groups, **21**
exploration, **24–25**, **26**, 28

famous people, **19**, **33**, **42**, **43**
film industry, 35, 37, 38, 42, 43
fish, 27
flowers, 14, 23, 37
food, 27, **40**, **45**

Golden Gate Bridge, **6**, **31**
gold, 22, **23**, 30, 31
Google, **39**
governors, 18, 19
The Great Wall of Los Angeles mural, **34–35**, **43**

Hollywood, 7, 35, 37, **38**

jobs, 32, 33, 38

languages, 26, 45
laws, 18, 19
Los Angeles, **7**, 35, 36, 37, **38**, 43

manufacturing, 32, 38
maps, **6–7**, **10**, **26**, **28**
Mexico, 29, 30, **45**
mining, 22, 30
Mount Whitney, 10, 12

name, 25
national government, 20, 42
national parks, **11**, **44**
Native Americans, 21, **26–27**, 28, 29

Pasadena, 37

population, 9, **10**, 20, 21, 44

recipe, **40**

Sacramento, 17
San Diego Zoo, **7**
San Francisco, **31**, 36, **37**, 39, 43
settlers, 26, 28–**29**, 30
Sierra Nevada mountains, 12, 22
Silicon Valley, **39**
Spain, 17, **24–25**, 28, 29, 30
sports, **36**, **41**, **43**
state government, 18, 20, 42
statehood, 31
symbols, **22–23**

timeline, **30–31**
topographical map, **10**
Transcontinental Railroad, **32**
trees, 11, **14**, **23**, 45

U.S. Congress, 20, 42

wars, 31, 32
writing, 35, **42**

Yosemite National Park, **11**

About the Author

Lauren Newman is a school library media specialist at a middle school in Columbus, New Jersey. She holds her bachelor's degree in English education from the College of New Jersey and her master's degree in library and information science from Rutgers University. This is her third book. Lauren's family lives in California, and she likes to visit the Golden State every chance she gets.